A Piece Of M.E

HAYLEY GREEN

DEDICATION

This book is dedicated to the UK Charity Invest In ME research and all of the volunteers, even though mostly unwell themselves, who dedicate their time and energy into running the charity.

The clinical trial fund for the drug Rituximab (appropriately nicknamed 'Hope in a bottle' by the charity, themselves) has given so many M.E sufferers, including myself, vital HOPE, that we can, one day, get our lives back.

So thank you, IIME Charity. You are just what we so very much need.

ACKNOWLEDGEMENTS

Thank you to every M.E sufferer who has been able to take the time and energy to write a poem to be included in this book.
In doing so you are helping to raise much needed awareness and funds for medical research.

All Fixed Up With Mefix Again
By R. Amor

I thought I was doing so well
it's such a shame
For now my body's had another breakdown
And I've found myself all fixed up with mefix again

It's so easy to slip
And find yourself with an intravenous drip
I hardly seemed to do nothing
But I guess I must have done something
to find myself all fixed up with mefix again

Still at least the bonus side to going out with ME
is you need spend nothing on booze, sex and crack cocaine
To find yourself with a massive hangover in intensive care next day
All fixed up with mefix again

Some days the sky is clear, my body vital and alive
Others it showers down with insomnia, IBS and pain
And no matter how hard I try to steer my life
I soon find myself all fixed up with mefix again

Sometimes I wonder if my body's too broken to be mended
Faced with everything it has to contend with
Yet still I struggle on along with my parents to whom I'm attended
Whilst I'm all fixed up with mefix again

A Piece Of M.E

Here I stand,
I think and fail,
I wobble on my feet.
I close my eyes
and take a breath
I'm pale as a sheet.
The tremors pass
The waves subside
The spasms start to slow
I hide a yawn
 And fake a smile
This is the life I know.
I fight the fog
And wipe the tears T
he dreams I once had, gone.
My body drags
My mind escapes
This evil curse has won.
And so I slip,
I've fought, I've failed,
I'm dragged under the spell
I can't break free
And so, I sleep,
Trapped in this living hell.

By Peyton Izzie Connor

Sometimes I look into the mirror
And see the life I could've had
One where I'd be thinner
And I wouldn't look so sad
Where my skin would be so clear
And my hair would be so sleek
My smile would be a real one
As my face won't feel too weak
My makeup would be flawless
Not riddled with mistakes
My eyes full of life there
Not a chore to be awake.
 I think that I'd be happy
No troubles on my mind
But portals to the mirror world
Are impossible to find.

By Peyton Izzie Connor

A Piece Of M.E

I look in the mirror and what do I see?
A girl who looks a bit like me.
She has my hair colour,
But Oh! What a pallor!
Am I really so pale,
Or was I just swallowed by a whale?
In my dreams I'm someone else,
Full of life, my good old self.
Simple things I'd love to achieve
Things other people complete with ease.
If taking a pill would make it go away,
Would I not take one of them today?
I am not lazy, I'm not just tired,
It's not in my head or just conspired.
Do I have the strength to go out?
Most days that is one big doubt.
I learn to pace, to take my time,
My head is full of constant rhyme.
My words mix up, my thoughts not clear,
Others think "Oh you poor dear".
I won't give up, I won't give in!
My life is different, but I will win!
No matter what, I am alive,
Me/CFS can take a dive.

By Hannah Gilmour

Hayley Green

"I'm down at heel
And out of life,
A has-been on the shore.
Once, dangerous to know,
Alas, no more!"

By Elaine English

A Piece Of M.E

"Whispers will turn to voices, and voices will turn to screams.
Screams will turn to action, and action will always mean...
Our whispers have been heard, the voices have spoken, people have talked and fought for the many hearts and bodies that have been broken."

By Chloe

Closed Thoughts?

My arms won't work
My legs won't work
Nor my brain.

You tell me it's psychological
Belief, depression, stress, emotion,
I don't know.

I go to lift my arm,
To open a jar,
To use a muscle.

It doesn't respond.
Can't or won't?
The blockage may be due

To my brain, thinking it can't.
Or maybe there's a chemical,
Lacking, a muscle impeded

A virus, a leakage of the battery
A wonky metabolism
A physical cause.

Whatever the reason
The connection fails
The brain and muscle do not engage.

I am not Uri Geller.
The Jar remains closed.

By Elaine English

A Piece Of M.E

It is morning and exhaustion
Creeps up my limbs and numbs them.
I lift my arm to greet the day,
It flops back, a useless member.
A few hours later I try again,
This time I succeed in getting out of bed
And making it down the stairs
Sitting, I ponder the weather outside,
I have no energy yet to contemplate breakfast.

Mid morning I am eating my breakfast.
I read the headlines of the newspaper
Before re-climbing the stairs:
My next hurdle.
I run the bath water
Switch on the iron to iron a top.
Later, relaxing in the warmth
My limbs are part of me again.

Resting again on my bed
I contemplate getting dressed,
Disguising my pallor
With make-up.
At last I am ready to face the day!
It is mid-day, most have moved on
From 'Good morning' to 'Good afternoon'.

Up and in the running,
I drive to work eager to show that
I still have something to offer.
Drained a few hours later
I crawl home
Wondering at
My lack of humility.

The next day I face the same mountain.
My limbs cry out at the abuse
I am putting them through.
The farce continues.
The days in between forgotten
In the mist of pain and lost words.

By Elaine English

When all the world is grey,
From the window of your soul,
May there come to you
A glimpse of golden ray
Escaping from the leaden sky
With promises of a brighter day.

You alone can give voice
To the mysterious world within you.
Can name the shapes and spaces
Can light a flame of love
To grow in your small space.

By Elaine English

Awake

Sleep evades my body,
But tiredness seeps through
My mind and limbs.

Walking, zombie like, through mists of time
Dull brain activity,
I wander in the corridors of my mind.
Dreams are welcome relief to this
Nightmare, no mans land.

I open the door and smell
Fresh day smell.
Cool air and birdsong
Awake my senses,
Briefly escaping
This painful assault
Of tired ceaseless repetition.

By Elaine English

Comic Poem

I want to write a funny verse
be acclaimed for my wit,
but my muse has deserted me ,
and all that I am left with,
is this.

By Elaine English

Changed World

Hole of despair;
Words have no meaning.
To describe a feeling,
Random electrical impulses?
And chemical reactions.
Perhaps, to call them instead,
Holes of opportunity?
Or mystery?

Unknown, unknowing.
Waiting to be discovered.
Catalytic reactions,
Bringing about change
To another zone.

To shift the focus,
Release the chemicals
Interpret the stimuli differently.
A scientific experiment.
Oh happy day!

I walk on water a dozen times a day
Achieving the impossible,
Negotiating
Between immutable forces
Beneath our consciousness.
Seeing differently
The world is changed.

By Elaine English
A Piece Of M.E

No Picnic

They've all gone out Lord
packing a picnic
lots of excitement
putting their boots on
calling the dogs up
clanging the gate shut
leaving me here

I want them to go Lord
don't want to deprive them
Why should they stay here
stuck in the house

Better to stride out
race down the footpath
leap over ditches
tramp through the bracken
run in the meadow
climb up the hillside
right to the top

Give me the strength Lord

not to be envious

not to feel lonely

but to be glad now

that I have You

When they come back Lord

help me to greet them

hear their adventures

laugh at their jokes

Don't let them know Lord

just how I feel Lord

how much I long for

when I'll be well

Help me to bear it

think of the good things

scent of the blossom

song of the blackbird

A Piece Of M.E

sun on the dew

and above all Lord

while I am waiting

help me to value

time spent with You

The Greasy Pole (or Life with ME)

My life now is one hard game

of climbing up the greasy pole

Inch by hard won inch is won

by weeks of rest and self control

Up and up, five yards I walk this week

and next month maybe even ten

But no…

I drop a cup and clear it up

or wrap a parcel, kneeling on the floor,

or visitors will stay too long (I love to see them)

or keep me, kneeling, talking at the door

All silly things, that no-one else thinks twice of

enough to send me speeding down the pole

to start that slow hard climb again…

again…

But one day surely I will reach that goal
A Piece Of M.E

Alone at Christmas

Alone at Christmas!

No, I had not thought so soon, Lord

Maybe in some far distant time when old and gnarled

Death had robbed me of my loved ones

And Death was near -

Not now …

Yet in the dusk

Beside the flickering candle flame

Before the crib,

I feel You here, with me

And I with You

So many busy families will forget You, Lord,

Your special day

Not I, this Christmas

Thank You, Lord

© Veronica Jones c 2000

A Piece Of M.E

(Written my first Christmas alone after husband had left, mum had dementia, and I was too ill for visitors)

Pain In My Heart

Does the pain outweigh the pleasure ? Does the pleasure outweigh
the pain ?

If I were to re-live my life, would I do the same again ?

I pushed myself so very hard, was never kind to me

Cared for everyone around, but no-one cared for me

The hurt that was being done to me I buried deep inside

The pain that I was suffering I found easy to hide

I smiled, I laughed, got on with it, the rock in everyone's life,

Me doing all the loving , but no-one loving me

No-one thought I needed help, a shoulder just to lean on,

Inside I was dying, but outside still just smiling

Now the hurt is back to haunt me, it seems I'm not so tough

The pain has now got physical, and I've just had enough

A Piece Of M.E

By Vickie Reeves 15th October, 2009

Hayley Green

KINDNESS PLEASE

COULD YOU JUST BE KIND TO ME?

I FEEL SO ILL, YOU SEE

TO YOU I JUST LOOK NORMAL

BUT THIS IS NOT TO BE

AN EVIL MONSTER DEEP INSIDE

HAS TAKEN ALL MY STRENGTH

I CANNOT EVEN BRUSH MY HAIR

NOR WASH MY FACE, AND CLEAN MY TEETH

HOW CAN THIS BE? I HEAR YOU SAY

YOU LOOK JUST FINE TO ME

PLEASE BELIEVE ME WHEN I SAY

I'M JUST NOT WHAT YOU SEE.

DOLLY APRIL 2013

A Piece Of M.E

INVISIBLE

WHY CAN'T YOU SEE THE AGONY I GO THROUGH EVERY DAY?

GOT FLU,FEEL SICK, IN SO MUCH PAIN

SO MANY SYMPTOMS, CAN'T EXPLAIN

I FEEL SO VERY, VERY, ILL YET I CANT TAKE A SINGLE PILL

WHY DON'T YOU THIS OR THAT THEY SAY

I DO, BUT IT WONT GO AWAY

DO THEY THINK I HAVE NOT TRIED?

IF I WAS NOT SO BRAVE INSIDE

BY NOW I WOULD HAVE SURELY DIED

TO THOSE WHO LOOK AND STILL CAST SCORN

I SAY BUT JUST ONE THING

PLEASE DONT JUDGE YOU JUST DONT KNOW THE AGONY I'M IN

IF YOU COULD HAVE THIS ILLNESS FOR EVEN JUST ONE DAY

INSTEAD OF POURING SCORN ON ME, YOU WOULD TAKE A DIFFERENT TACK

AND WISH WITH ALL YOUR HEART, THAT VICKIE COULD COME BACK

Hayley Green

BY VICKIE REEVES

A Piece Of M.E

Bluebells

In a sunlit wood not far away

Under trees where rabbits play

A fragrant blue carpet is laid each year in May

The beauty to take your breath away

Singing, dancing in the warm spring breeze

Peeping at you from beneath the trees

The fragrant Bluebells lift your heart

As you breathe their scent so deep

No one can take this beauty from you

It is yours to love and Keep

By Vickie Reeves

Hayley Green

Alone

I walk alone on ancient shores

Long since lost at sea

Where time and space will ebb no more

Nor all things lead to me

Dreams lost and yet to come no more

Bear down without emotion

Every atom every fibre

Demanding my devotion

The shores will strangely echo

As I stand like frozen stone

In time alas outside itself

I walk this path alone

Vickie Reeves – Nov 2012

A Piece Of M.E

THE BUTTERFLY

WHERE IS THE GIRL WITH THE SMILE ON HER FACE

WITH SPARKLE IN HER EYES

AND LAUGHTER IN HER VOICE

SHE IS NOT LOST FOR EVER

JUST HIDING FOR A WHILE

SOME TIME IN THE FUTURE NOT TOO FAR AWAY

SHE WILL EMERGE FROM SLEEPING

TO LIFT YOUR HEART AGAIN

THERE IS NO TIME FOR SORROW

FOR TEARS OR DESPAIR

IT IS ENOUGH TO HEAL HER

JUST KNOWING THAT YOU CARE

A BETTER PERSON WILL EMERGE

LESS VAIN – LESS SELF AWARE

SOON WILL COME THE BUTTERFLY

Hayley Green

SOARING HIGHER IN THE AIR

EVER STRONGER AND FAR WISER

WITH LESSONS LEARNED FOR LIFE

BY VICKIE REEVES

A Piece Of M.E

Springtime

Tiny buds on tiny trees,

Tiny flowers, tiny leaves,

In my garden life awakes,

I sit outside without a care,

The breeze whispers as it moves my hair,

I rest and feel the sun at last,

No more dark shadows winter casts.

The birds all sing in sheer delight,

An end to hardship now in sight,

Another winter we've survived,

M.E. has not dimmed our light,

Our hearts still strong, our spirits bright,

Renewed our strength to bear our plight.

By Vickie Reeves

Snowfall

Is there anything more gentle and pretty than snow as it falls to the ground?

The beauty is truly astounding as it casts brightness and light all around.

Soon the children are playing and laughing, it's clear that they like to have fun

Better be quick with the snowman, before it goes with the warmth of the sun

The old folk, though, do not like it. They whinge and they whine and they moan

Better stay in while it melts then, you're safe in your home, so stay warm

By Vickie Reeves

Ripped Apart

I FEEL SO SMALL AND HELPLESS, VULNERABLE AND
WEAK

LIKE A TINY KITTEN IN THE JAWS OF ROTTWEILERS

RIPPED FROM LIMB TO LIMB

THEY WILL SHOW ME NO MERCY, JUST TOSSING ME
AROUND

FIRST THROWN FROM SIDE TO SIDE

THEN SMASHED IN TO THE GROUND

NO ONE COMES TO SAVE ME

SO INNOCENT AND SMALL

I PLEAD AND BEG FOR MERCY

BUT NO ONE HEARS MY CALL

DOLLY. APRIL 2013

Me and my M.E.

I'm sitting on the ground

at the bottom of the Well

and I'm getting pretty tired

of this endless M.E. hell

And I'm thinking to myself

That things don't look too bright

And the light that shines above me

Is fading from my sight.

I've been to see the Doctors

I've taken all the pills

I've read the books

and joined the Groups

And now I've had

my fill.

I'm tired of all the 'payback'

I'm sick of 'foggy brains'

of throbbing legs

and aching heads

and pain. And pain. And pain.

But most of all I'm angry

at all the days I've lost
through lack of Notes and Research
- WE pay the brutal cost.

Of hope? There has to be some.
That distant light must shine.
So strain your eyes
before it dies
to glimpse it, down the line...

By Sue Tame

Shadows

Silver crescent in deep night sky
Spreading light on the earth
Now fading behind a veil of cloud
Radiance depleted.

Ghostly image, life-in-waiting
Hoping for shadows to clear
To reveal the brilliance and energy
Of silver crescent in deep night sky.

By Vivienne Waldron.

On Reflection

In the still of the afternoon
When sun streams through the window
And crystal reflections bounce on the walls
Birdsong falters
Distant traffic quietens
And memories flow
Rise and fall
A murmuration of starlings
Filling the sky
Wheeling swirling patterns
Of light and shadow
Faces and voices
Long forgotten
Rushing to greet me
In the still of the afternoon

By Vivienne Waldron

Dressing Down – M.E Style

I had the feeling I was letting you down

Going to the theatre in my dressing gown

It should, at least, have been the good one

Not the grey fleece with the bobbles on

But it didn't seem to matter to me at all

Though I remember feeling a little small

In my slippers, slothering down the centre isle

Like a slug gliding over a patio tile.

When I took my seat in the front row

I heard those around me whisper, "Oh, no!"

Unperturbed, I settled myself down

In my shabby, comfy old dressing gown.

The lights went down, the curtain rose

The leading man opened his mouth....and froze

He stared at me, in his dumbstruck state

"Come on, get started," I said, "You're late."

A Piece Of M.E

When I woke from my dream I felt quite vexed

Not knowing just what happened

By Vivienne Waldron

Curtain Up

It is the muted light of early morning:

The land is shrouded in mist and an unearthly silence

The sombre stillness of waiting

It is almost time

Almost time for curtain up

That moment when the audience holds its breath.

Now that first glimpse of the stage

As the greyness lifts

To reveal a rural scene

Hedges and tree tops appear

Garbed in gold and brown, red and orange.

Act one and the players enter

The herald sings his introduction

And opens another tale

But you, dear reader, are no mere watcher

For you are making your own story

Every day.

A Piece Of M.E

By Vivienne Waldron

.

The silent scream that no-one hears, my pleas for help fall on deaf ears,
No-one understands the pain, my battle within, exhaustion reigns,
Push myself harder, just do some more, my body aches, my muscles sore,
Don't let it win, don't let it beat me, but my body still defeats me.

No rest days, just requests for me to assist, even as my body grows weaker,
No energy to fight, I can't say no, the pain inside grows, my future looks bleaker.
You don't look ill, I hear them say, but they only ever see me on a good day.
Do too much, I pay severely, in pain and torment, it costs me dearly

. Others don't see the price I pay, just to get me through the day.
They don't see me crawling on the floor, unable to stand, and bang into doors
, Too weak to hold a spoon and eat some food, this illness is so misunderstood. Brain fog and shaking, are part of the deal, a sickness from which I can never heal.

Walk too far, my legs give way, shots of pain radiate the rest of the day.
Too tired to breathe, too tired to live, never get any relief.
Spend my days on the toilet, with stomach cramps from food I regret.
A soak in the bath or a lie in won't fix me, total rest and relaxation is my only therapy.

Oh no, I cannot indulge that selfish act, I know how they would react.
My silent scream, it's getting louder, I'm going crazy, but they just think that I am lazy.
It's all in your head, get out of bed, push yourself through it, you can do it!

A Piece Of M.E

Suffer for trying, end up crying, in frustration and pain, then do it all again.

They want more, I must endure, suffering and pain, but can't explain
To deaf ears that don't want no excuses, if I have outlived my uses.
So silently scream, this life of misery, is mine alone, not allowed to moan.
Suffer in silence, they don't want to hear, the pain I must bear.

Pretend to be normal, pretend to be well, yet really life is a living hell.
Gotta pull my weight, mustn't be a burden, fix my face, with false smiling.
Just one more day, gotta get through it, relentless, endless, suffering and anguish.
They are lucky, they are happy, they don't know the reality of living with M.E.

By Maria Rogers

In the still of the afternoon
When sun streams through the windows
And crystal reflections bounce on the windowsill
Birdsong falters
Distant traffic quietens
And memories flow
Rise and fall
A murmuration of starlings
Filling the sky
Wheeling, swirling patterns
Of light and shadow
Faces and voices
Long forgotten
Rushing to greet me
In the still of the afternoon.

By Vivienne Waldron

The Window Pane

The window's view
Won't break my pain
Won't put my shell
Back together again.

The blood soaked rose
Won't fill my heart
Won't send my story
Back to the start.

The candied clouds
Won't cure my sorrow
Won't keep my faith
From feeling hollow.

The swooping Jackdaw
Won't lift my spirits
Won't take my hand
And pull me with it.

The auburn sun
Won't erase my grey
Won't re-set This Groundhog Day.

By Joanna Cocco

My Dungeon

My body is my dungeon
Jailing me with pain and exhaustion
Nausea and weakness complete my rack
Which is ever ceaseless in its attack

I watch my life washing away, day by day
Even my soul seems to be swept away
Fear and grief cripple my spirits
My mental state is pushed to its limits

Even sleep is rare to ease my suffering
Nor people to give care and comforting
No key is there for this jail I'm in
No treatment for this state of sin

Loneliness is my constant companion
Disrespect my only medallion
For not only is there no cure
Misconceptions I must also endure

My brain is a swirling sea of fog
Around me all is black as smog
But despite all this I still search for a light
The liberator that will end my torture

By R Amor

No 2 Birds in Your Heart

Have the birds
of your heart
deserted you,
gone away and left you?
Have the songs of your heart been silenced?
Do not fear.
If asked
they will return; These
heart birds need
only to be asked.
Create a space;
Nature abhors a vacuum
. Call the birds to the aching
and one day they will return to you,
and sing in the morning
and through the day,
and at night,
and even at times,
Call the sun,
the moon,
and the stars;
To shine
for you.

By Jonathan Eyre

Hayley Green

I'll tell you about M.E.

I'll tell you about M.E.
Write down your dreams, your
aspirations, on a sheet of paper,
Done it?
Write your aspirations down.
One or two of them, maybe the
deeper ones.
Done it?
Now tear it up,
tear up the sheet of
paper with your aspirations written
down on,
Tear the sheet of paper into tiny
pieces and throw them to the floor.
Commit littering where you are
now, don't hold back!
Done it?
Do this every day, every hour, in
the street, in your seat, in your car, in your kitchen, in your bed, do
it where you stand,
where you cook,
where you think, at the work desk, on
your computer..
Not just mentally but in this
physical representation of your
personal dreams for a future.
This is the process of M.E.
Torn dreams, aching limbs, and an
exhaustion that strips you of your souls
desires, strips you of your

A Piece Of M.E

simplest objectives in life,
Tears even the thoughts you are
having at a moment in time,
Tears the conversations from your
mouth as you are trying to have t
hem, Tears them into shreds.
So you make your dreams smaller,
I've read the books,
done the
Cognitive Behaviour Therapy
'patient sufferers' course.
You make your aspirations easier to achieve,
To go and post a letter
To read the next few pages of a
novel
To say hello to a friend...........
And I can see you have not got it..
Go on, write these smaller dreams
down on a new piece of paper
Now tear them up throw them to
the wind, these simpler dreams, Do this every hour;
train your mind to accept this
To accept that even the shadows
of your deepest dreams are torn to
shreds,
Rendered into a fatty deposit that
sinks to the bottom of the latrine of
your aspirations. That there is
around you the smell of festered
and decomposing dreams......
Your life is not broken, it is torn
over and over and over again,
Thrown as confetti the day you
became shotgun wedded to this
disease
And you now find these torn pieces
hidden in the clothing of
your personality, the folds of your
character

Turning up as decapitated words
and scrambled torn individual
letters On thousands of pieces of torn
sheets of paper;
Shards spirited away by unseen
underground rivers of illness
And I see you might be getting it.
The enormity of this incurable
disease that cheats on the body,
steals the mind and toils the
soul....
So now that you are working it out,
write these thoughts down on a
sheet or paper
and tear them up to smaller pieces
and send these to your friends
I have no need of them, I have too
many of them of my own.

By Jonathan Eyre

Up Down Spin Sit Down

Up, down, spin, sit down
the dizzy cycle doth surround
my every day, can wear me down
I keep fighting on because I'm proud

Proud of achievement big or small
have a bath or to answer the door
dream of a walk or bloody well do
it
everyday I'm fighting through it
It's just the surface people see
I so want folk to understand me
those people skills are evading me
I so miss those I no longer see

It's not sympathy that I seek
but it's apathy that makes me weak
I'm sure you life is full and busy
but spare a thought for one lost
and dizzy

By Colin White

Hayley Green

Chronic Fatigue Syndrome

Just because you can't see it
Doesn't mean it isn't there
Into the existing perimeters I don't
fit
It seems like you just don't care

The doctors I go to make me feel crazy
Not validated in my suffering
I'm exhausted and my head is
hazy
I never know what tomorrow will bring

You say to exercise and sleep
You don't understand I feel frail
My sanity is up to me to keep
This is my journey, my tale

There are others who feel like me
The same set of symptoms I feel
We all couldn't be crazy
But more days of our lives you
steal

What could a psychiatrist do?
I didn't make up chronic fatigue
syndrome

A Piece Of M.E

It started after I had a flu
It's left me alone, struggling and
home

This isn't the life I want to live
I want to be out and about
Something's gotta give
Soon
they will figure it out

I know you won't apologize
You think you know more then me
I just hope someday you realize
I was right and you couldn't see

I'm only depressed because I feel
ill
If I didn't have this sickness I'd be
okay
I don't need you to offer me a pill
I'll stay strong and be on my way

By Jennifer Bering

Walking into Forever

If she could let you inside
You wouldn't find your way out
She has to pretend and hide
Pushing away every doubt

You might last a day
And think it's not so bad
But when this is your new way
You'll beg for the life you had

She has to be made of stone
Use what she can to survive
You'd hate to feel so alone
Somedays not think you're alive

You wouldn't make it long
You'd want to give in
She's been doing it so long
She waits for her rebirth to begin
In order to keep going
You have to keep starting new
Living without knowing
If this will someday end for you

You might think she's weak
That you could do better
If this nightmare is what you seek
Join her and you can walk
together

By Jennifer Bering

The Existence

Wanting to run away
Not living, just existing
In this body I cannot stay
This illness is exhausting

Every cell of my being
Energy has stopped renewing
My eyes have trouble seeing
My body, trouble moving

The more I try to do
The worse its effects on me
Symptoms start out with a few
Turning into many

My strength is depleting
Any extra movement makes it
worse
My spirit, this illness is defeating
How can I stop this curse?

Feeling winded, need to lay
I know I've overdone
I hate feeling this way
It wasn't even doing anything fun

How much more?
When is the end?
What's in store?
When will my body mend?

Perseverance is a must
maintaining faith and hope
My body feels like it's going to rust
Each day I fight the tears to cope.

To all of this there is a dark side

It's called FOREVER
It's something from which I hide
For that sentence is too much of an endeavor

How will I stay strong
Day after day, Year after year
All my plans went wrong
I've felt down, lived with fear
Dreams put on hold

Wishing I didn't have to
My heart gets so cold
Only way I know to make it through
How do you tell yourself no?
it's not in the cards, not for you.

Don't let Emotions show
smile and pretend it's not true My
body is living
Lungs breathe, a heart beat
My soul is existing
Hoping for more, feeling defeat.

By Jennifer Bering

Hopeful and Free

In my dreams
I run like the wind I can soar, I can fly
In reality I wonder if I have sinned
Why living my life, would you
deny?

I often feel afraid
It's lonely and unplanned
Broken plans and promises made
For I'm too tired to stand

I try and try
Never giving up hope
Sometimes I cry and cry
And mope

It's hard to be strong
Days go by all the same
Wondering how long
Will we play this game?

I want to wake up and go about my
day
Not a worry in my mind
I can do anything I
want or say
The beauty in the world is out
there for me to find

I know I am still me
I am funny, kind and smart
Thankful for those who let me be
You will always be in my heart

Positive I must stay
For it is better then its alternative
I know that there will come a day
When I can get back out there and
live!

By Jennifer Bering

Another Day

My house is a prison
Days that I cannot escape
Not well enough to drive
How will I mentally survive?

Reliant on others
Most often I need to be taken out
Can't just go as I please
Need to put my mind at ease

The thought of these 4 walls
Suffocating all life inside
Pretending it's alright
Convincing myself I'm winning this
fight

No freedom to be me
Fun and free spirited
Waiting to see how I wake up
As to, is it half empty or full my
cup?

So I spend another day frustrated
My mind wants to go out on my own
Body says to stay in
Another day my mind will win!!

By Jennifer Bering

The Prison

Somewhere along the way her fortress became a prison. No bars of steel, just the restraints of her mind.

Locking her in and the rest of the world out.

No less real because they could not be seen by the naked eye, or touched by the flesh.

They were there in her head, and no matter where she looked, or how hard she tried, the key to unlock them could not be found.

It eluded her as did the love, peace and contentment she craved.

Nobody came in and she could not leave. The longer she remained imprisoned the lonelier she became.

The windows giving her a glimpse of the outside world, and letting some much needed light into the darkness of her thoughts.

Enough to keep the fire in her heart flickering, but not yet powerful enough to make it burn.

No passion, no fight, just acceptance that the girl with the sparkle in her eyes and the zest for life, is lost in the fog and is yet to return.

By Saire Dubois-Scott

A Piece Of M.E

I often turn your invites down
rarely see me out in town
think that I'm a little flakey
always sleeping never wakey
s'pose you think that I'm boring
rather spend my life snoring
take it easy laying in bed
you can't see inside my head

can't imagine the pain I feel
I'm not faking, its for real
I know you think I look ok
but I'm hurting every day
I'll get up if I can
it takes the strength of Superman
every morning that I wake
I feel every muscle ache

its like when you have the flu
my every day is like that too
on top of that I get brain fog
it's like a nasty mental smog
It slows down my normal thinking
It's like feeling I've been drinking
I really have to plan my day
in such detail, in every way

if I use up too much energy
it will be the end of me

it will be my Kryptonite
i'll have no power left to fight
go to bed, hit the sack
wake up early with 'Payback'
And payback just doubles your
pain
so on my settee I'll remain

for another long and lonely day
hoping the aching goes away
watching crap on television
feeling like I live in prison
Longing to meet up with you
and to do the things you do.

By Michael Scott

My Bed, My Prison

My carer and my keeper.

Punished for I know not what
Shackled to my mattress,
A quilt of little comfort hides
My constant pyjamas.

My bed, my sentence
Seems longer than forever.
Staring at these white four walls
In a bed of isolation,
Wishing for a cell mate
For a two-way conversation.

My bed, my saviour
My tormenting torture chamber.
Curtains mask my iron bars
Flowers keep on calling,
The punishment for picking them
Bones of lead come morning.

Hayley Green

My bed, my body
Is aching for an answer.
My lawyer says there's nothing left
To cure my situation,
Just keep on lying on your slab
And pretend it's a vacation.

By Joanna Cocco

A Piece Of M.E

When sun streams through the window

And crystal reflections bounce on the windowsill
Birdsong falters

Distant traffic quietens

And memories flow

Rise and fall

A murmuration of starlings

Filling the sky

Wheeling, swirling patterns

Of light and shadow

Faces and voices

Long forgotten

Rushing to greet me

In the still

of the afternoon.

Vivienne Waldron

A few hours later I try again,

This time I succeed in getting out of bed

And making it down the stairs.

Sitting, I ponder the weather outside,

I have no energy yet to contemplate breakfast.

Mid morning I am eating my breakfast.

I read the headlines of the newspaper

Before re-climbing the stairs:

My next hurdle.

I run the bath water,

Switch on the iron to iron a top.

Later, relaxing in the warmth,

My limbs are part of me again.

Resting again on my bed

I contemplate getting dressed,

Disguising my pallor

With make-up.

A Piece Of M.E

At last I am ready to face the day!
It is mid day, most have moved on

From 'Good morning' to 'Good Afternoon.

Up and in the running,

I drive to work eager to show that

I still have something to offer.

Drained a few hours later

I crawl home

Wondering at My lack of humility

The next day I face the same mountain.

My limbs cry out at the abuse

I am putting them through.

The farce continues,

The days in between forgotten

In the mist of pain and lost words.

This book is dedicated to Phyllis Rose
Briginshaw
1921 – 2017
Forever In Our Hearts

ABOUT THE AUTHOR

Hayley Green is a Severe M.E Sufferer based in the UK. Previous publications include:

'101 Tips for Coping With M.E'

'What Is M.E? A Guide For Children. Explaining The Illness In A Way Children Can Understand '

'Understanding M.E, A Guide For Friends Family & Carers'

'Tickle ME – Stories Of A Brain Fogged Girl'

'Life With M.E – Words Of Warriors'

'Meet M.E'

All books donate 100% of royalties to Invest In M.E Research

Printed in Great Britain
by Amazon